In the Name of God, ¨

God of Verbs Vs

All Righ

MuslimSchool.com

ISBN: 9798297773370

Imprint: Independently published

Manufactured in the United States of America

https://MuslimSchool.com

Publisher's Cataloging in Publication

Ghounem, Moussa Mohamed

God of Verbs Vs. God of Nouns: A Divine Trilogy

[Mohamed Moussa Ghounem]

1st ed.

p. cm.

ISBN: 9798297773370

1. Quran --Relation to the Bible. I. Title.
2. Islam --Relations --Judaism. II. Title.
3. Islam --Relations –Christianity. III. Title.
4. Bible scholars – Jewish scholars – Muslim Scholars

Interfaith Love memo: This series speaks truth to ideas, not condemnation to people. It challenges beliefs, never bloodlines; doctrines, never dignity. It invites honest, respectful dialogue — the kind that builds bridges where walls once stood.

Dedicated to: Al Hagg Moussa Elsied Ghounem (Allah Yarhomuk) And Tito

Contents

Commencement by our 3 Guides

In the Name of God, the Most Gracious, the Most Merciful.

To the seeker holding this book:

Health be upon you. We are a Rabbi, a Sister, and a Sheikha—custodians of three sacred streams from one Divine source.

For centuries, many of our children have stood on opposite banks, believing the other rivers to be foreign, even hostile.

But we have been blessed to witness a journey—the journey of a single, broken, and lovely soul named Selah, who was brave enough to drink from all three of our streams. Her story taught us what our hearts always knew but our minds had sometimes forgotten: that the God of Abraham, Moses, Jesus, and Muhammad, peace be upon them all, has always spoken one language.

It is the language of action. The grammar of verbs.

This is not a book to be read with the mind alone. It is a scroll to be walked with the soul. Walk slowly. Walk in verbs. And may you arrive, as Selah did, not at a new religion, but at your own truest, most ancient, and most beautiful self.

May you arrive whole — healed where you were torn, lit where you were dim.

With love that does not fade,

Rabbi Elara, Sister Joan, and Sheikha Imani

Preface

In the beginning was the Word, and the Word streamed across history.

Imagine God's covenant was not a book bound in leather, but a signal of living light streamed directly to our heart—A Divine Trilogy in three Seasons—A Spiritual Love Series that heals the world.

Season 1: The Calling. In a world of tribal chaos, a voice calls for a different kind of strength. A law is given to protect the orphan and defend the widow. A command is issued to love the stranger as yourself, for you were once strangers. A covenant is made not just of fire and stone, but of verbs that demand justice and build a community of compassion. Starring: *Abraham, Moses, Pharaoh, the Burning Bush*

Season 2: Finding Love. From the dust of Galilee, a carpenter comes, speaking verbs of radical love. He heals the untouchable, eats with the sinner, and washes the feet of his own followers. He tells a world built on power to love its enemies and declares that the kingdom of God belongs to children. He is a verb of pure mercy, breaking every wall that divides the human family. Starring: *Jesus, Mary, Pilate, the Roman Empire*

Season 3: Universal Loving. The Series returns, confirming all the love that came before and sealing it for all time. A command is given to never harm your children, to protect the orphan, and to defend the widow. A Prophet teaches that God shows no mercy to one who shows no mercy to the young and that saving a single life is like saving all of humanity. Starring: *Muhammad, Jibreel, Khadijah, the Quraysh*

The Big Reveal: You have heard of Jews for Jesus. But what if there were Muslims for Moses and for Jesus? There are. We are. This epic is the bridge, welcome to A Divine Trilogy. Faith is not a title you claim. It is a verb you become, a light you embody for the world.

Introduction: The Grammar of God

A crisis has quietly spread across the religious world, dimming the light in countless hearts. It is not atheism or secularism, but a sickness more subtle: entitlement. A generation has inherited labels without labor, covenants without contracts, and faith without function.

The sacred name of God has been used as a noun to be possessed, rather than a verb to be lived. Across continents, wars are fought over the noun "chosen," and billions claim Abraham's inheritance while few embody Abraham's obedience. This series was born in opposition to that dangerous grammar. It is a rescue mission for faith.

Somewhere along the great, flowing river of revelation, we built dams of dogma and began to worship the stagnant water. We were given verbs of radical love— *to go, to heal, to serve, to read, to submit* —and we froze them into nouns of tribal identity.

The holiest expressions of God became badges to be worn, titles to be possessed, and borders to be defended. The mission became a monument. We inherited the names of the Prophets but abandoned the pattern of their footsteps, creating a museum of fossilized faith where we polish the exhibits of "Jew," "Christian," and "Muslim" while the living spirit within them aches for motion.

This book proposes a new theological lens, **God of Verbs Vs. God of Nouns**, which rediscovers a pattern long buried beneath dogma: that God, in every Scripture, favors obedience over ancestry, verbs over names, and action over identity.

But a Divine Trilogy of this magnitude cannot be understood through argument alone. It must be felt. It needs a heartbeat.

Episode 1: The Trembling Verb

The heartbeat is a woman named Selah. Her awakening is not a gentle drift from slumber but a sharp, clean break. There is only the immediate, pressing grammar of duty. Her feet find the cool floorboards with a practiced silence as she moves into the kitchen.

The crisp fold of her apron feels unnervingly like the starched collar of her old uniform. She wonders if every heart carries a secret wound — a moment of irreversible loss that no soul, soldier or not, can ever undo.

Her hands, strong and capable, move with a precision that borders on the sacred, but a fine tremor lives within them—not the weakness of age, but the persistent aftershock of a soul that has witnessed what no soul should witness. It is the body's prayer for peace, written in a language only the broken understand.

It is the body's refusal to forget what the mind tries to bury, a kind of holy *ra'ad*, the trembling that took the mountain at Sinai, now contained in the cage of her own ribs.

She measures oats, slices a banana, and arranges her mother's medications in a small ceramic bowl—the white pill for the heart, the blue for the pressure, the pale yellow for the sorrow that has no name. Each action is a verse in a silent psalm of care.

This is her *mitzvah*, the holiest of commandments. It is the one remaining thread connecting her to the covenant, the last pure action in a life she feels is irrevocably stained.

She carries the tray into her mother's room. Her mother is awake, a fragile silhouette against the morning light. Selah helps her sit up, plumping the pillows behind her. As she feeds her mother the warm oats, spoonful by spoonful, her mother's hand, frail and cool, covers her own trembling one on the bowl.

"The shaking is loud today," her mother says, her voice a soft, rustling whisper. It is not a question, but a statement of fact, of shared witness.

Selah nods, unable to speak.

"A beginning," she whispers, her voice carrying the weight of ancient wisdom and tender prophecy, "is God's favorite thing. He is always making them—in the breaking dawn, in the cracking seed, in the breaking heart. *Especially* in the breaking heart."

The words are a small, unexpected gift. A single, perfect verb in the midst of her stagnant nouns. Selah holds her mother's gaze, and for a moment, the roaring static in her own soul quiets to a hum. To feed her mother, to be seen by her—these are not just acts of love; they are her anchor in a churning sea of chaos. This precision is a shield, a carefully constructed wall against the disorder that rages within her.

In the quiet rhythm of this care, she is not a broken thing. She is a daughter. She is a verb.

Episode 2: The Synagogue of Welcome

The quiet precision of the morning psalm has faded. By late afternoon, the Jerusalem light, once soft and forgiving, has hardened into a brassy glare that offers no corners for hiding. The tremor that lived in Selah's hands has escaped, and now it riots through her whole being. It is a familiar storm, a violent shaking that begins in the soul and demands to be stilled by the old, familiar poison.

She is on the floor of her bathroom, the cold tile a small anchor in the churning sea of her craving. Her mind, desperate for order in the chaos, focuses on a single, hexagonal tile, tracing its six perfect sides with her eyes, over and over. But the geometry offers no peace. In her hand is a small orange bottle, the forgotten pills of a prescription from a time she has tried to bury. The plastic cap clicks as she twists it, a sound as loud as a gunshot in the silent apartment. Her mind, her soldier's mind, supplies the rationale with brutal efficiency:

Just one. To still the shaking. To quiet the ghosts. You have earned this peace. No one will know.

This is the moment of surrender. The verb she knows best. Not submission to God, but to the void. She tips the bottle, her thumb poised to release a single white pill into her palm.

And then, a different voice. Not a command, but a whisper, faint and fragile, from a lifetime ago. It is her mother's voice, from before the sorrow took up permanent residence. Selah is a child again, feverish in her bed, and her mother's cool hand is on her forehead. The memory comes with the scent of chamomile and the weight of a blessing, whispered in Hebrew into the whorl of her ear:

"Y'varechecha Adonai v'yishmerecha… May God bless you and keep you…"

The memory is a clean, sharp blade of light that cuts through the filthy logic of addiction. The blessing asks for God to *keep* her, to *guard* her. The pill offers only oblivion. A dry sob escapes her throat — the sound of a soul tearing itself in two. With a final, desperate act of will, she hurls the bottle. It strikes the far wall and skitters under the sink, out of sight. The ghosts rage, but for now, they are denied.

She pulls herself to her feet, her body slick with a cold sweat. The vow is not a grand pronouncement; it is a ragged gasp for air. "I will go," she whispers to the empty room. "I will turn."

The doors to the Kehilat Nitzan Synagogue are heavy, carved from dark, unyielding wood. Selah's hand hesitates, her fingertips brushing the cold grain. The faint scent of old books and beeswax drifts out, mingling with a ghostly memory of her father's prayer shawl, a scent of wool and quiet faith. "I don't belong here," she whispers to herself, but a child's giggle from inside, bright and unjudging, pulls her forward. She steps in.

The air is warm, alive with the murmur of the evening prayer. She slips into a seat in the back row, her head bowed. After the final *"Amen,"* as the small congregation begins to disperse, a woman approaches. It is Rabbi Elara.

"Shabbat shalom," the Rabbi says softly.

Selah flinches, taking an involuntary half-step back, her body's muscle memory of retreat kicking in before her mind can stop it.

The Rabbi's eyes, the color of warm honey, notice everything and judge nothing. "It is good to have you with us," she says, her voice calm and even.

"I… I don't belong here, Rabbi," Selah stammers, the words tasting like ash. "I am… not clean."

Rabbi Elara's gaze holds no pity, only a deep, intelligent compassion. "You have been taught that holiness is a noun," she says gently. "A state of perfect purity you must arrive at, spotless. But our tradition teaches something far more merciful."

The Rabbi leans a little closer, a flicker of wit in her warm eyes. "The Torah gives us a beautiful, secret verb. *Teshuvah*. The world translates it as 'repentance,' a single, heavy monument to our failure. But that is not its heart. The true verb is *lashuv*. It means *to turn*. It is a pulse, not a verdict. A direction, not a destination. You do not *arrive* at holiness, my child; you *pulse* toward it, a river bending toward the sea. God does not demand you reach the shore. He only asks that you keep your heart aimed at the music of the ocean."

Selah looks up, her own eyes stinging with unshed tears.

"*Teshuvah* is not a state of being," Rabbi Elara continues. "It is a continuous verb of turning. God does not ask that you arrive without dust on your feet. He only asks that you keep turning toward Him. The turn itself—that is the sacred act. That is the proof of the soul's life."

For the first time in a decade, Selah feels a warmth spread through her chest that does not come from a bottle. It is a flicker of hope, a candle lit in the vast, windy darkness of her soul. The Rabbi is not offering an absolution Selah cannot accept. She is offering a direction she can take. A verb she can live.

Later that night, Selah sits with her mother. The house is quiet. Her mother, lucid for a rare moment, turns to her.

"You were out late," she says, her voice clear. "Did you find what you were looking for?"

Selah, still processing the Rabbi's words, answers honestly. "I found a beginning."

Her mother smiles—the first real smile Selah has seen in years, a flash of the woman she used to be. "Good," she whispers, her eyes shining. "Beginnings are God's favorite things. He's always making them."

Episode 3: The Burden of Chosenness

A fragile peace has taken root in Selah's soul. The verb *lashuv*—to turn—has become her daily meditation. She turns toward the morning light, toward her mother's needs, toward the quiet wisdom in Rabbi Elara's study. For the first time in years, she feels a sense of belonging that is not forged in conflict. But peace in Jerusalem is a temporary truce, and the grammar of the city is relentless.

She's walking home, the simple act of buying bread a small, grounding ritual. The warm, yeasty scent of a fresh challah in her bag is a comfort. Her path takes her near a checkpoint, a permanent scar of concrete and steel. Her new heart sees the wound of it, the cold grammar of power. A young Palestinian woman argues with a soldier, her voice tight with frustration. Selah's eyes are drawn not to the argument, but to the baby strapped to the woman's chest, its tiny hand clutching the fabric of its mother's scarf, a small, perfect fist of innocent trust in a world of walls. The universal vulnerability of it pierces Selah's armored heart.

She forces herself to look away, only to walk past a cafe. She catches a snippet of a heated discussion.

"...it is our right. God gave us this land," one man says, his voice thick with certainty. "We are the chosen. They need to understand that."

The word hangs in the air. *Chosen*.

The word '**chosen**' strikes Selah not as theology at all, but like the blunt end of a rifle slammed into her chest. She recoils, stumbling back a step, knocking a small table. A cup clatters to the ground. She mutters an apology, gathering herself while her hands shake with a deep moral revulsion. The word from the man's lips sounds exactly like the word "elite" from the mouth of her former commanding officer. It is the sound of a wall being built.

A cold fear snakes around her fragile hope. Is this faith just another uniform? She enters the Rabbi's study, the turmoil a live grenade inside her.

"Rabbi," she says, her voice raw with the bluntness of the battlefield. "I heard a man today use the word 'chosen' like it was a weapon. Is this faith just another tribe that builds its walls and despises everyone on the other side? Because I have worn that uniform. And it almost killed me."

The Rabbi nods slowly, her eyes sad and validating. "Good," she says, her voice a balm. "Your anger is righteous. It is a sign your soul is awake." She guides Selah to the heavy Torah scroll. "Let us leave the slogans of the street and go back to what God's word actually *says*."

She unrolls the parchment. "Let's begin where God began. With Abraham. Please, Selah. Read this."

Selah reads the familiar words from Genesis: "...and all peoples on earth will be blessed through you." She stops.

"The first promise," the Rabbi says gently. "What is its stated purpose?"

"To bless... everyone," Selah whispers, the surprise evident in her voice.

"Exactly. It does not begin with a wall. It begins with a river. But Rabbi," Selah pushes back, her voice gaining strength, "if it's a river, why do so many people build dams with it?"

"An excellent question," the Rabbi affirms. "Let's see what the prophets say." She guides Selah to Isaiah. Selah reads, "I will also make you a light for the nations..."

"A light," the Rabbi repeats. "Is a lamp's purpose to admire itself, or to shine so that others may see?"

"But they *do* use it to admire themselves!" Selah insists, the fire returning. "They use it to feel superior!"

"And our own prophets raged against that corruption," the Rabbi says, her voice firm. "Look here. Amos. Read it slowly."

Selah leans in, her voice a whisper as she reads the devastating words. "'You only have I chosen of all the families of the earth… *therefore*, I will punish you for all your sins.'"

The word lands like a thunderclap. *Therefore*. The logic is inverted, the pride shattered. Selah looks up, her eyes wide.

The Rabbi leans forward, her gaze tender. "Is chosenness a shield that protects you from God's law?" she asks softly. "Or is it a burden that binds you to it more tightly than anyone else?"

Selah cannot answer. The word she heard on the street has nothing to do with the terrifying, beautiful, and demanding verb she sees written here. She is left in a state of profound, stunned silence as the epiphany washes over her: the horror of a holy verb of responsibility being twisted into a profane noun of privilege.

Later that week, she is at the interfaith food drive. The gathering is a symphony of cooperation—women in hijabs, men in kippahs, a young Christian priest from an Ethiopian Orthodox Church with rolled-up sleeves, all working together. Selah is packing bags when a small girl, a Syrian refugee with eyes that have seen too much, tugs on her sleeve.

"Why do you pack the rice so tight?" the girl asks, Selah looks at the bag in her hands, her movements precise, tactical, efficient. She looks at the child. And for the first time in years, a genuine, unbidden laugh escapes her lips. It's a rusty, unfamiliar sound.

"Force of habit," she says, a real smile reaching her eyes. She loosens her grip, letting the bag settle more gently.

As she hands the bag to the girl's mother, their eyes meet. *This,* Selah thinks, a thunderclap in her soul. *This is the verb. This is the light. Yet just as the feeling crests, a familiar ghost flickers at the edges of her mind. A backfiring truck cracks like gunfire; cold dread knifes into her fragile peace. In an instant, the hard-won light shatters. One desperate question rises from the depths of her soul: I'm finally living the right verbs — so why does my soul still ache?*

Episode 4: The Unspoken Wound

On the surface, Selah is a study in healing. She lives the verbs she has learned with a soldier's discipline. She *turns*. She *serves*. She *acts*. From the outside, the broken vessel appears to be mending. But inside, the static is growing louder.

She is standing in the Synagogue, wrapped in the warm, communal hum of the Shabbat service. The congregation rises to sing. Selah's lips form the words, her voice joining the chorus.

—A sharp, metallic click of a magazine locks into place—The phantom sound slices through the prayer. Her voice falters. The warmth of the room recedes, replaced by a sudden, bone-deep chill.

Selah's eyes lose focus, her vision tunneling until the prayer shawls in front of her become the drab-uniforms of her unit. She blinks hard, her breath a ragged gasp, and the Synagogue rushes back into view. Her heart hammers against her ribs.

The righteous verbs are not enough. The community's warmth cannot reach the frozen core of her trauma. She feels like a fraud, a ghost haunting a life of faith. The stain, she feels, is not a surface impurity; it is woven into the fabric of her soul. One evening, after a harrowing night where the ghosts screamed louder than her prayers, she knows she needs something more powerful. A verb of total immersion. A spiritual flood to wash the wound itself. Her mind seizes an ancient, radiant image: the Mikvah.

She goes to the living waters, her heart a knot of desperate hope. As she steps into the pool, she whispers a prayer, a plea. *Please let this be enough.* She immerses herself once, twice, three times, letting the water cover everything. But as she rises, the water clings to her like a shroud of ice. Her skin prickles with gooseflesh, not renewal. The wound—*her* wound—hasn't even rippled under the surface.

She returns to the Rabbi's study, a city hollowed out. "I did the verb of purification, Rabbi," she says, her voice a hollow echo. "I went into the water. But the stain didn't wash away."

The confession lands in the quiet room, a stone sinking into still water. Rabbi Elara's heart aches, her own eyes glistening. She takes Selah's ice-cold hands. "Selah, the Mikvah can wash the world from your skin. But some sorrows sink deeper than water can reach." Her voice catches, a rare tremor in her steady wisdom. "Our Torah is beautiful, eternal, but it was not written for the shrapnel of modern souls. This wound… a shadow that lingers in the soul's quiet corners, it is a moral injury. And to heal a memory…" She trails off. "That may require a different kind of verb."

The Rabbi leans forward. "Perhaps, before God can heal a wound, we must first have the courage to read its verses aloud to Him." Her gaze is an invitation of absolute safety. "The text we must read now, my child, is you."

Selah's breath catches. Her hands grip the arms of the chair. A wave of dizziness washes over her. All her life, she was trained to bury this text.

"I can't," she whispers, the words catching on a knot of terror.

"Just one line," the Rabbi says, her voice a lifeline. "The one that haunts you in the quiet."

In the sacred space between them, Selah closes her eyes. Her voice is a raw, ragged tear in the silence. "There was a boy… He couldn't have been more than fourteen. His eyes… they were so wide…" A dry sob chokes off the words. She has read the first verse.

Later that night, Selah sits in her apartment as Jerusalem settles into its ancient rhythm of evening prayers. From her window, she can hear the distant call to Maghrib, the bells of a Church, the murmur of Jewish prayers. Three rivers of praise flowing to the same ocean, and she—despite all her turning, all her verbs—remains stranded on the shore.

She closes her eyes and allows herself to name the unnamable. The words escape her lips in a whisper she has never dared speak aloud. Not to the Rabbi. Not to the therapist. Not even to God.

"I killed a child."

The weight of it sits in her chest like a stone that no ritual water can dissolve.

"He had a gun, but his hands were shaking worse than mine. I had a split second to choose, and I chose to let his mother lose her son so that some other mother wouldn't lose her daughter."

The tears come now, a flash flood that has been building behind a dam for years.

"The Torah says 'You shall not murder.' But what do you do when obedience to one command means breaking another?"

She opens her eyes and looks out at the city where Abraham almost offered Isaac, where Jesus walked, where Muhammad prayed on his night journey. This city that has seen every kind of faith and every kind of failure.

"Maybe," she whispers to the darkness, "the wound isn't what I did. Maybe the wound is believing I can't be forgiven for it."

The thought settles over her like a thin blanket—not warm enough, but better than the cold.

Episode 5: Forgiveness (Season 1 Finale)

When Selah enters the Rabbi's study for the last time, the air is different. She is not a student today. She is a condemned soul walking to her sentencing. All the soldier's defenses have fallen away, leaving only a raw, hollowed-out stillness. She sinks into the chair, her body moving with the heavy, final weight of a stone sinking into deep water.

Rabbi Elara looks at the young woman before her, and her heart breaks. The flicker of hope she had so carefully nurtured in Selah's eyes is gone, replaced by a vast and desolate emptiness.

"The stain," Selah says, her voice a dead, flat whisper that seems to absorb all the light in the room. "It's not a memory, Rabbi. It's me. It's what I am. I thought if I did enough good verbs, I could… paint over it. But it's in the marrow. It's in every breath I take. I am the ghost. I am the walking wound. I am the thing that cannot be cleansed."

The confession is absolute. It is a verdict she has passed on herself.

The Rabbi listens, and every word is a blow to her own heart. A single, silent tear escapes the corner of her eye and traces a path through the fine lines of her face—a tear not of pity, but of a shared and unbearable sorrow for this child of her community. She reaches across the table and takes Selah's trembling, ice-cold hands in her own warm ones.

"Selah," she begins, her voice thick with a love that is maternal, ancient, and absolute. "Everything you have done—your turning, your service—is beautiful in the eyes of God. You are a beloved daughter of this covenant. Nothing can ever change that." She squeezes Selah's hands. "But the path of *Teshuvah*, the map I have spent my life studying… it is for sins against the law."

The Rabbi takes a deep, steadying breath, and speaks the hardest and most loving words of her life. "My child, I do not have the words for a wound this deep against the self. The map of our fathers is beautiful and true, but it does not have a name for the shrapnel in a modern soldier's soul. I have reached the edge of my map. And I love you too much to pretend it is the whole world."

Selah walks out of the Synagogue and into the blinding Jerusalem sun, a ghost in her own life. Adrift, she walks without direction until she finds herself in a small, crowded cafe near the Jaffa Gate. From a nearby Church, bells toll softly, their rhythm foreign yet strangely beckoning, like a verb she cannot yet name.

Through the fog of her despair, a conversation from a nearby table cuts through the noise. Two men, their faces etched with a weariness she recognizes, are speaking English. They are veterans. The word "unforgivable" hangs in the air, and a memory flashes in Selah's mind—a comrade, after a mission gone wrong, offering a quiet, simple absolution she couldn't accept.

The older veteran leans forward. "It's not about getting the world to forgive you," he says. "It's about finding a way to grant yourself a radical, personal forgiveness. Especially for the unforgivable."

The phrase struck Selah with the force of a physical blow. *Radical, personal forgiveness for the unforgivable.* It is a grammar so alien her mind stumbles. She unconsciously touches her throat, the place where her own confession is stuck. It is not hope; it is a profound and disorienting shock, a flash of lightning that reveals, for a split second, the outline of a door she never knew existed.

Back in the quiet solitude of her apartment, a deep, aching gratitude for Rabbi Elara rises in her heart. *Thank you,* she whispers to the evening air. *Thank you for showing me the edge of your map.*

She pulls out her phone. The small object feels impossibly heavy, a tool of immense spiritual weight. Her thumb hovers over the cool glass, her hand shaking with a profound and holy fear of the unknown. *Turn, she said,* Selah thinks. *But where do I turn when the wound is me?*

Her resolve hardens. With a final, decisive movement, she opens the search bar. Her fingers, slow and deliberate, type the words from another universe.

Veterans support group Jerusalem.

She hesitates, then adds another word.

Forgiveness.

She presses search.

The screen flickers, and then a list appears. One of the results mentions a group that meets in the basement of a Church. A list of names, of places, of possibilities written in a new and unknown language of healing.

As she stares at the glowing screen in the dark, a single, silent tear of terrifying hope traces a path down her cheek. The journey was not over. A new and unknown sea awaited.

Season 2: Finding Love to Love

Episode 6: The First Step

The hallway of the Jerusalem community center was a sterile, impersonal purgatory, lit by the unsteady hum of yellowing fluorescent lights. The air smelled of old linoleum and disinfectant. Selah stood motionless before a plain wooden door, a ghost haunting the space between her past and a future she could not imagine.

Her hand was raised, but it was frozen. This was the terror of a soul split between two impossible commandments: the duty to the past and the desperate need for a future. Her entire being felt shattered. She clutched her phone, the screen displaying the words that had led her here:

Veterans support group Jerusalem. Forgiveness.

Turn back, a voice screamed inside her, a voice of loyalty to Rabbi Elara, to her father's memory.

This is a betrayal. But it was a beautiful, holy map, and she had reached its edge; her soul was still lost in an uncharted, violent sea. Another voice, a whisper from a stranger's conversation, offered the only direction she had left:

…radical, personal forgiveness. Especially for the unforgivable

. This was the last, desperate instinct of a drowning woman clutching at a rope she could barely see.

She took a ragged breath. I will go. I will turn. The verb *lashuv*, the turning toward God, propelled her into this new, terrifying current. Her fingers finally closed around the doorknob. The click of the latch was a sound of finality, and she stepped across the threshold.

The room was a simple circle of mismatched chairs, a secular space that allowed Selah to slip into a seat in the back, her posture coiled, ready to flee. When it was her turn to speak, a silent shake of her head was her only offering, and it was accepted without judgment. The focus shifted to a veteran in his fifties named David, a witness testifying to a wound she recognized as her own.

"The shame... that's the ghost that doesn't leave," he said, his voice raw. "It tells you you're unclean. Unforgivable." Selah flinched. "I tried everything," he continued. "Good deeds, therapy, prayer... They gave me tools to live, but they couldn't wash the stain from the inside." "Then someone told me to stop *thinking* about God and start *reading what Jesus did*. And the words weren't about doctrine. They were verbs. Radical verbs." His voice grew quiet with awe. "This man... He didn't just talk about love;

He touched the unclean. He ate with the sinner. He was a **verb of pure mercy** in motion. He offered a forgiveness that wasn't for the righteous, but for the broken. For the shattered."

Selah felt the words bypass her mind entirely; it was a testimony she could not deny.

That night, she paced her small apartment, a caged animal. David's words echoed relentlessly:

a verb of pure mercy. Her gaze fell on her Torah scroll with a wave of profound, heartbreaking love. It was a **"perfect vessel"** of Divine law, a sacred **"light"** that had guided her. But she accepted a truth that felt like a blade of loving honesty: this **shrapnel of a modern soul** was a pain the sacred map could name but could not heal. This was not a betrayal. It was the ultimate proof of the very *teshuvah* the Torah had taught her, a **"continuation"** of her turn toward God.

She pulled out her father's old wooden chest and found it at the bottom: a small, worn copy of the New Testament. She saw herself with a sudden, shocking clarity. She was not a conqueror. She was a **"refugee from her own condemnation,"** seeking asylum.

In this quiet, desperate act, her **"tremble was a prayer. Her desperation... a beatitude."** With a final, ragged breath, she opened the cover, beginning the holy act of **"uncovering the unity behind"** all revelation. Her journey into a new and unknown sea had begun.

Episode 7: "The Radical Verbs"

A few days had passed since Selah first opened the New Testament. The initial, terrifying hope had curdled into a thick fog of confusion. She had been reading, but the words were a jumble of foreign names, strange parables, and a timeline she couldn't grasp. The man from Galilee felt less like a verb of pure mercy and more like a historical ghost, wrapped in layers of theology she could not penetrate. She felt lost, a seeker with a broken compass.

The bus ride to Beit Hanina was a study in tension. Her hyper-vigilance, a soldier's faithful sentinel, scanned every new face, every stop. The Hebrew on the signs gave way to Arabic. She felt her otherness like a heavy coat, her muscles coiled. Her mind churned, trying to make sense of her reading. *The words of Matthew blur like a map in a storm—names, parables, no clear objective. Is this mercy or madness?*

Driven by the memory of the veteran's raw testimony, she had chosen a humble listing from her phone: "The Little Sisters of the Common Good." This was not the act of a potential convert. This was a soldier on a reconnaissance mission deep in what felt like enemy territory.

The address led her not to a Church, but to a simple, functional building of Jerusalem stone, fronted by a sprawling, productive community garden. There was no steeple, no cross on the door. Instead of solemn quiet, the place was a hive of activity.

She stepped inside and the scent of vegetable soup and antiseptic filled the air. In one corner, two women were packing food boxes. In another, a young man tended to an elderly man's bandaged foot. The sound of a hammer striking a nail echoed from a back room. In the midst of it all, a woman in a hijab, packing a box of dates, caught Selah's eye and offered a small, quiet smile—a wordless, unambiguous welcome. This was a place of verbs, not nouns.

A woman emerged from the garden, wiping her hands on a worn apron. She was in her sixties, with deep laugh lines and a smudge of fresh dirt on her cheek. This was Sister Joan. Her eyes, a startlingly clear blue, met Selah's and saw everything. She saw the soldier.

"Welcome," she said, her voice warm but practical. "Are you here for a meal, or to help make one?"

Selah, unable to answer, found a quiet bench near the garden. She held her New Testament like an unexploded ordnance. A few moments later, Sister Joan approached with two cups of tea and sat beside her. She looked at Selah's guarded posture, the tension in her shoulders.

"I once ran from the orders in that book, too," Sister Joan said softly, a gem of unexpected vulnerability. "I thought they'd break me. They didn't. They remade me."

Selah looked up, surprised. The Sister nodded toward the book.

"That book isn't a history text," she said, her voice gentle but firm. "It's a set of military orders for a different kind of war."

The line stunned Selah. It cut through her confusion with a surgeon's precision.

"You read it like a soldier," Sister Joan continued, her perception unnerving. "You're right to be confused. *Theology would have bounced off your armor. But orders? A soldier knows how to obey.* I am not asking you to 'believe' in peace; ... Consider this spiritual surgery... an elite special ops mission for the soul"

She leaned forward slightly, her gaze locking with Selah's. "The commands are the most difficult a soldier has ever been asked to follow." She began to list them, her voice clear and steady, each word a direct order.

"Heal." "Forgive." "Serve." "Love your enemy."

Selah retreated to a secluded corner of the garden, her heart hammering. The Sister's words had unlocked something, and now her mind was a battlefield where two grammars collided in a terrifying, electrifying clash.

Old Grammar: **Neutralize the threat.** *New Grammar:* **Love your enemy.**

Old Grammar: **Maintain tactical superiority.** *New Grammar:* **Serve.**

Old Grammar: **Never forget, never forgive.** *New Grammar:* **Forgive seventy times seven.**

This was the violent deconstruction of her identity. Every instinct that had kept her alive was being challenged by a logic so radical it felt like madness. It was terrifying because it meant the death of the soldier who had survived. It was electrifying because it was the first grammar that spoke directly to the wound of shame.

As she wrestled with the impossible new orders, a small cry broke her concentration. A young boy had tripped on the gravel path, his knee a mess of blood and dirt.

For a split second, Selah froze—the passive, wounded observer.

Then, without conscious thought, her training surged through her. She moved instantly, kneeling beside the crying child. Her movements were swift, economical, and infinitely gentle. "Shhh, it's okay. You're okay, soldier," she whispered.

As her hands, steady and sure, began to clean the small wound with a handkerchief, a sharp, visceral image flashed in her mind—a half-second memory of the **same hands, slick with sweat, gripping a rifle.**

The contrast was a physical shock. The soldier's instincts had not been erased; they had been re-channeled. The same precision once meant for harm was now being used for healing.

It was a small, simple verb: *to help.* Her first, unconscious step in obeying one of the new commands. She looked down at her own hands in stunned surprise, as if they belonged to someone else.

From across the garden, Sister Joan watched, a knowing, compassionate smile gracing her lips. The soldier, she knew, had just completed her first drill.

Episode 8: "A Covenant Divided"

A week had passed. A fragile, tentative peace had begun to settle in the fissures of Selah's soul. She had found a new rhythm, a life defined by the radical verbs she was learning to obey. Her days at the community were spent in a state of quiet discipline. She weeded the sprawling garden with a soldier's focus, served meals in the common hall with silent efficiency, and listened—truly listened—to the stories of the people who came seeking shelter or a warm meal. For the first time since before the uniform, she felt a sense of belonging that wasn't forged in conflict.

To deepen the fragile understanding that was taking root, she sought out Sister Joan. "Sister," she asked, "do you have something simple I can read? To understand more."

Sister Joan smiled, her eyes full of warmth, and returned a few moments later with a few well-meaning pamphlets and a slim, simply written book on the history of the Church. That evening, in the quiet of her small room at the community, Selah began to read. And it was there, in the cold, impersonal print of a chapter on the early Church Fathers where she first encountered the doctrine. A single word, at first. *Supersessionism*. Then, the explanation: the doctrine that the Church had "replaced" Israel as God's chosen people, and that the Jewish covenant was now obsolete.

The book fell from her hands. The words on the page were not abstract theology; they were a direct, personal assault. A cold dread seeped into the room, leeching the color from the fragile peace she had so carefully cultivated. She looked out her window at the vibrant community, but now it seemed different. The kindness she had received felt tinged with pity, the gentle welcome a gesture extended to a relic of a dead and broken faith.

She retreated into herself, the pain a white-hot nova in her chest. *This doctrine, this single idea, invalidates everything.* It invalidated her father's memory, turning his quiet faith into a tragic dead end. It invalidated the brilliant, eternal light of the Torah that had been her first guide.

And most painfully, it invalidated Rabbi Elara. It twisted her guide's profound wisdom into a folly. It meant the Rabbi hadn't lovingly led her to the edge of a map; it meant she was a keeper of the *wrong map* altogether. This doctrine took her entire past, the Jewish identity she had just begun to reclaim and honor, and turned it back into a fossilized "noun"—a thing to be studied in a museum of dead religions. The sense of betrayal was absolute and overwhelming.

Sister Joan found her hours later, sitting on the same garden bench as before, but this time she was a fortress of ice. The sister's gentle greeting was met with a stony silence. She sat beside Selah, her presence a patient, questioning warmth. Finally, Selah turned to her, her face a mask of grief and fury.

A sharp, painful memory flashed in her mind, as vivid as the present moment: *the Rabbi's warm study, the scent of old books, and Elara's gentle voice saying, "Our covenant, Selah, is a sacred, unbroken chain stretching back to Sinai."*

The memory made the words in the book a direct violation of that sacred trust. With the blunt honesty of a soldier, she held up the book, her voice dangerously quiet.

"Rabbi Elara told me our covenant was an unbroken chain. This book says you came and broke it. Is that what you believe?"

Sister Joan did not flinch. She met Selah's pain with complete, validating stillness. Her own face filled with a deep, historical sorrow.

"Yes, that doctrine is in our history," she said, her voice aching with shared pain. "And it is a wound. Not just a wound that my tradition inflicted on yours, but a deep, festering wound in the heart of our own family. A sin of pride we have answered for and must continue to answer for."

Her solidarity was disarming. As Selah processed this, another thought, clear and sharp, rose from the wisdom she was absorbing: *So this is what it is. Not a holy doctrine, but a human one. A theological tribalism.*

Sister Joan continued, her voice gaining a firm resolve. "It had to be faced. **Because humility must be a verb, Selah—an active, continuous choice. The moment it becomes a noun, a badge**

we claim, it transforms into arrogance. And for centuries, we chose the noun."

She paused, then said, "Let's go back to the original orders." She opened a worn Bible to **Matthew 5:17** and asked Selah to read it aloud.

Selah's voice was hoarse. *"'Do not think that I have come to abolish the Law or the Prophets; I have not come to abolish them but to fulfill them.'"*

"That word," Sister Joan said, tapping the page. "Fulfill. Our pride twisted it into 'terminate.' Our fear turned it into 'replace.' But that is not what it means." She looked at Selah, her eyes luminous with a fierce, loving intelligence.

"Selah, to **fulfill a seed is not to destroy it, but to help it grow into the tree it was always meant to be. To fulfill a promise is not to erase it, but to see it come true in its most glorious form.** Jesus came to show us the full, loving expression of the Law's heart—to take the verb of righteousness and show how it blossoms into the verb of radical love."

A weight Selah hadn't even realized she was carrying lifted from her soul. Later, she walked back into the community's common area, her perspective shifted. This place was not a replacement; it was a continuation.

Her eyes fell upon a scene near the tea station. The woman in the hijab was sharing a loud, happy laugh with an elderly Jewish man, a kippah on his head, who often came for a warm meal. The theological "divide" had closed in her heart.

In a final, quiet act, Selah poured a fresh cup of hot tea. She walked over to the Jewish man, holding it out to him. As her hands extended the cup, a sharp memory surfaced—a half-second flashback to those same hands, years ago, trembling uncontrollably as she reached for a pill bottle. Now, they were perfectly steady.

The elderly man looked up, his eyes kind and knowing, and he took the cup. He looked at her, truly saw her, and offered a simple, powerful blessing in return.

"May the God of Abraham bless you, my child."

The words washed over her, a balm on the wound she thought would never heal. As she stood there, her heart overflowing, a series of thoughts bloomed in the quiet of her soul.

He doesn't see a stranger. He sees a child of Abraham. The law isn't gone... it's blossoming into love.

And then, a final, healing grace note, as if whispered on the wind from another garden, she heard Rabbi Elara's voice in her heart.

"She did not steal my student; she honored my teachings and returned my daughter to me, whole."

Episode 9: "The Word Became Verb"

A newfound stability had settled into Selah's days. It was the quiet equilibrium of a soldier who, having survived one war, was now finding her footing in a new, unfamiliar peace. She had accepted Jesus as a teacher of radical verbs and had healed the wound of the divided covenant. As a daughter of the Torah, she felt she was not converting, but continuing her journey, following the radical, embodied love of the Nazarene as the ultimate verb of the God she had always known.

Her studies with Sister Joan had moved from the earthy, direct commands in Matthew, Mark, and Luke to the more poetic, philosophical waters of the Gospel of John. It was there, in the very first verse of the first chapter, that she hit a wall. It was a wall so solid, so absolute, that it stopped her heart cold.

She read the words:

"In the beginning was the Word, and the Word was with God, and the Word was God... And the Word became flesh and dwelt among us."

The sentence was a barrier of pure granite. After all her progress in moving from static nouns to living verbs, she had crashed into the biggest, most immovable "noun" of all.

She retreated, deeply disturbed. The community, which had become a safe harbor, now felt alien, its core belief a danger to her soul. As she sat alone, a sharp, poignant memory ambushed her. *She is a little girl, her hand held firmly and lovingly in her father's as he points to the mezuzah on their doorpost. He says gently, "In here, Selah, is the Shema. 'Hear, O Israel: The LORD our God, the LORD is one.' It is the first and last truth. It is our heart."*

The memory made the words in the Gospel a direct violation of that sacred, loving inheritance. Her mind, her soul, was reeling. *How can a man be God?* This was the very thing her ancestors fought against. It felt like a spiritual betrayal. Was this the price of healing her own wound? To abandon the one, absolute truth her father had placed in her heart? It felt as though she had been led down a beautiful path that ended abruptly at a cliff of idolatry.

Sister Joan found her later in the small, quiet Chapel. Selah was standing before the simple wooden cross on the wall, staring at it not with reverence, but as if it were an enemy position she was trying to understand before dismantling it.

"Sister," she began, her voice tight with pain and confusion. "I can follow the verbs—heal, serve, forgive. But this... 'the Word was God'? Sister, my soul knows only one God. There are no others."

Sister Joan did not answer immediately. She simply stood beside Selah, sharing the silence. When she finally spoke, her voice was incredibly gentle.

Selah, the English word 'Word' is a tiny, wooden box for a Greek idea that is a forest of living light.

The original word was *Logos*. To the ones who first heard it, *Logos* was the Divine blueprint, the cosmic reason, the underlying grammar that holds the stars in their courses and teaches the tide when to bow.

It is the operating system of reality itself... So let us read it again. Not as 'the Noun became a person.' But as 'The Divine Action took on a human life.' 'The Creative Syntax was written in flesh and blood.'

'The very Verb of God learned to walk and to weep.'

The words landed, one by one, like keys turning locks deep inside Selah's soul. "Jesus wasn't a noun that replaced God," Sister Joan concluded, her voice now a near whisper. "He was the ultimate verb of God, entering the world to show us the pattern in a way we could finally see and touch."

Selah stared at the cross, but she no longer saw an object of idolatry. The contradiction that had been tearing her apart didn't just resolve; it evaporated. Christology, the great wall of nouns, was suddenly reframed through the lens of verbs.

She turned to the sister, her eyes wide with the luminous peace of a profound epiphany.

"So," she whispered, the words catching in her throat, **"the Word is not God's name. It is God's *doing*."**

And in that moment, she felt a strange resonance, a memory of Rabbi Elara speaking of the Torah not as a book, but as God's Divine Blueprint, the creative wisdom that existed before the world. This new idea didn't feel foreign... it felt like a long-lost cousin to a truth she already knew.

Later that evening, in a final act of embodied grace, the community gathered for a simple meal... Her hands—the hands of a soldier—were now performing the ultimate radical verb. She was not just understanding the Logos; she was, for the first time, helping to embody it.

Selah saw the elderly Jewish man from the previous day, his face tired. She watched as Sister Joan knelt before him with a basin of warm water, unwrapping the clean bandages from his feet to tend to them.

Before, Selah would have seen this as a kind act. Now, she saw the unconditional love for God's creation in motion. She saw the Divine Spirit being expressed not in a sermon, but in the humble, powerful actions of this woman.

After a moment of watching, Sister Joan looked up and met Selah's eyes. She didn't say a word, but simply nodded toward the basin of water and the clean linen—a silent invitation.

Selah hesitated for only a heartbeat. Then she moved, crossing the room and kneeling opposite the sister. She took a clean linen cloth and, after Joan had washed the man's other foot, Selah began to gently dry it.

Episode 10: "The Limits of Grace"

A quiet rhythm had taken root in Selah's life, a peace woven from the steady verbs of service. She worked in the garden, her hands finding solace in the soil. She served meals in the common hall, her presence a calm anchor in the room. She was at peace. But she knew, with the certainty of a soldier who can feel the storm before it breaks, that the core wound remained—a pocket of shrapnel deep in her soul that no amount of good work could dislodge.

One afternoon, she found Sister Joan sitting on the stone bench by the rosemary bushes. She approached with the directness she knew the sister would understand, the economy of a soldier with a clear objective.

"Sister," she began, her voice low and steady. "You taught me the verbs. Now I need to use the hardest one. Forgiveness." She took a breath. "But for myself. I need you to guide me. I'm ready to face it."

Sister Joan looked up, her gaze full of a profound, loving gravity. She had been waiting for this. She simply nodded, stood, and led Selah toward the small, quiet Chapel. This was not for a formal confession. This was for a guided, prayerful confrontation with memory itself.

Inside the Chapel, the air was cool and smelled of old stone and beeswax. There was no judgment here, only stillness. Sister Joan didn't offer easy absolution or empty platitudes. She guided Selah to sit, to close her eyes, and to walk back into the memory that had haunted her for years.

"See it, Selah," the sister whispered. "But this time, see it through the eyes of God's radical mercy."

And so, Selah spoke. For the first time, the whole story came tumbling out, the words jagged and raw. The heat, the shouting, the confusion. The split-second decision.

"...he couldn't have been more than fourteen," she choked out, tears now streaming down her face in a silent, violent storm. "He had a gun, but his hands... his hands were shaking worse than mine. I chose to let his mother lose her son so that some other mother wouldn't lose her daughter. I chose..."

"What did you choose, Selah?" Sister Joan prompted gently.

"I chose to kill a child," she sobbed, the words tearing from her throat, finally uncaged. The full weight of the confession settled in the quiet Chapel.

"And what does Grace say to the one who did that?" the sister asked softly.

Selah wept, a deep, shuddering catharsis that shook her entire body. Through the storm, Joan's voice was a steady anchor. Finally, after an eternity of tears, Selah's breathing steadied. In the ensuing quiet, she heard the final, gentle prompt.

"What is the verb you need, my child?"

In a whisper so faint it was almost silent, Selah finally said the words to the only person who needed to hear them. She said them to the broken soldier inside her.

"I forgive you."

It was a profound, soul-shaking release. A tectonic shift deep within her spirit. And in that moment of grace, as she saw her own face in her mind's eye finding a sliver of peace, a fleeting, powerful vision appeared alongside it: **a flash of the face of the boy's mother, her eyes mirroring the same devastating pain Selah had carried for so long.** This vision was the seed. Her own forgiveness was now instantly and inextricably linked to the suffering of others.

In the quiet aftermath, sitting in the Chapel's gentle light, Selah was not just peaceful; she was transformed. The frantic energy that had propelled her for years was gone. The ghosts were quiet. But in their place, a new feeling rose—not doubt, but an overwhelming, aching love for humanity, born from the vision of that mother's face.

Her personal healing had exploded into a universal compassion. The question that would define the next chapter of her life was born not from intellectual curiosity, but from a heart that had been broken open by love.

She found Sister Joan in the garden, her eyes shining with this new, holy fire.

"Sister," she began, her voice urgent with this new love. "If this message is true and this love is universal, why is it so complicated? Why is it wrapped in a story that half the world doesn't accept? Where is the final, unambiguous expression of this grace for all people, beyond culture, beyond interpretation?"

Sister Joan listened, her expression one of deep, sad wisdom. She smiled, a faint, loving acknowledgment of the purity of the question.

"Selah, that question is not a sign that your healing is incomplete; it is proof that it is perfect," she said, her voice full of a gentle, paradoxical truth. **"Perfect healing doesn't end the search; it begins the real one—the one for others."**

She paused, choosing her next words with care. "For me, the Gospel is the clearest, most perfect vessel for that love. It is the language my soul understands. But I cannot claim to know how God speaks to every soul across every age. My map can guide you to the Living Water, but I cannot claim it is the only river that flows to the ocean."

It was an answer of profound humility and honesty. As Selah heard it, a sense of awe filled her. *She loves my soul more than her own map... just as Rabbi Elara did.* The loving symmetry of her two guides, each willing to release her for the sake of her journey, was a breathtaking gift.

But a new search had begun—calmer, vaster, and even more profound.

Selah found herself in a new state of being, standing on a balcony at the community center that evening, looking out over the ancient walls of the Old City. She can see the lights of the Christian, Jewish, and Muslim quarters. She is not looking at them as a soldier assessing a tactical situation. She is a soul filled with a boundless love, looking out at the family of humanity. As she gazes at the three distinct expressions of faith, a final, clear question crystallizes in her heart, a quiet whisper that is now the thesis of her life:

"My wound is healed. But the world's wound is not. Where is the mercy that covers us all?"

She is healed, but she is not yet whole. Her journey is not over.

Episode 11: "The Unread Book"

The days that followed Selah's healing were filled with a quiet she had never known. The ghosts were gone. The frantic, pained energy that had propelled her for years had dissolved, replaced by a deep and abiding peace. She continued her work at the community, her hands finding a steady rhythm in the garden, her presence a calm reassurance in the dining hall. She was healed.

Yet, a new kind of restlessness pervaded her quiet moments. It was not the sharp edge of anxiety, but a calm, persistent, and expansive ache. Her mind, now free from its own war, constantly wrestled with the question that had been born from her healing: *Where is the mercy that covers us all?*

She would watch the beautiful, specific faith around her with a heart full of love and gratitude. She saw Sister Joan in the early morning light, her fingers moving across the beads of her rosary. She heard the gentle hymns sung during evening prayers. She recognized the profound truth and beauty in these rituals. But she now saw them with a gentle sense of detachment. She had been saved by this beautiful river, but her heart was now seeking the ocean.

Her quest for a universal answer, for the ocean itself, eventually led her beyond the loving confines of personal mentorship. If an answer existed that was meant for all humanity, it must live somewhere in the collected wisdom of the world. One clear, bright morning, her journey led her to the grand, quiet halls of the National Library of Israel.

The act of walking through its doors was a threshold crossing. The cool, silent air, the scent of old paper and limitless knowledge, was a world away from the Chapels and Synagogues she had come to know. This was a new phase. She was no longer just a patient being healed by the wisdom of others; she was now a researcher, an active seeker in charge of her own quest. She stood for a long moment in the main reading room, filled with a quiet awe, surrounded by the silent, waiting voices of history, philosophy, and faith.

She found her way to a towering section dedicated to theology and philosophy. She wasn't looking for a specific book. She simply let her hand trail along the spines, reading the titles, waiting for something to speak to her universal question. Her fingers stopped on a book titled *On Universal Ethics*. As she pulled the heavy volume from the shelf, her eyes caught the title of the book nestled beside it.

The Holy Qur'an.

She froze. Her hand recoiled from the shelf as if from a hot flame.

A sharp, visceral flashback ambushed her, pulling her from the quiet library to a dusty, tense briefing room. An intelligence officer is pointing to a slide. On the screen is the cover of a Qur'an, and the officer's voice is a cold, clinical drone: *"This is their playbook. Know your enemy."*

The memory hit her with the force of a physical blow. The book before her wasn't just a book; it was a threat profile. The wall she hit was made of concrete and razor wire.

She stood there in the silent library aisle, her heart hammering. The old soldier in her whispered warnings, words of caution and suspicion, fueled by the memory. It was the grammar of a world divided into "us" and "them."

But her new heart, the one that had been so tenderly healed, spoke louder. The soldier's voice of fear was silenced by a clear, compassionate question that rose from the very core of her new being: **"How can I seek a mercy that covers everyone if I refuse to even read everyone's story?"**

The question was the engine. It gave her the resolve to act. As her hand moved, slowly, deliberately, toward the book, a second realization dawned, a sense of awe at the nature of her own quest: *This is what Rabbi Elara meant. This is a magnificent, terrifying, Jewish question.* The thought connected this brave, frightening act back to her deepest roots. She was not abandoning her heritage; she was fulfilling its most profound command to pursue truth.

She took the book from the shelf. The act of walking to the checkout desk was a journey in itself, a quiet, momentous victory. As she walked, a final, clarifying thought defined the very nature of her action. *This is the hardest verb of all. To love your enemy... by daring to know them.* It was not an academic exercise. It was a spiritual act, the ultimate fruit of the healing she had from accepting Jesus.

Back in her simple room at the community, the evening light, soft and golden, filled the space. The Qur'an sat on the small wooden table in front of her. She was not reading it yet. She was simply sitting with it, her hands resting on the table, near the cover, a universe of possibility waiting in the quiet.

She looked down at her own hands. *These are the same hands that once trembled uncontrollably, now perfectly still.* The visual confirmation of her healing was absolute.

In this final moment of stillness, Selah felt something she could not yet name. It was not just peace. It was a gentle, inexplicable pull toward the book, a sense of being guided, a feeling not of choosing, but of being led home. This was the feeling of *Hidayah*, Divine Guidance, the perfect, unspoken bridge that would lead her into the heart of God's ocean.

Season 3: Universal Loving

Episode 12: "The First Recitation"

Selah is in her room, a sanctuary of stillness in the heart of a bustling community. The evening light has softened to a gentle lavender, and her hands, steady and sure, are resting near the unread Qur'an. She is at the threshold. The entire world seems to be holding its breath.

She has journeyed through the grammars of action and understanding. She has been healed. She has been remade. And now, the quiet, inexplicable pull of *Hidayah*—the Divine Guidance she could not yet name—urges her to take the final step.

After a long moment of profound stillness, a silent prayer of intention forming in her heart, she performs the next great verb of her journey: *to read*. She reaches out, her fingers tracing the elegant script on the cover before opening the book. Her eyes fall upon the first chapter, Al-Fatiha. "The Opening." She reads the simple, powerful words of praise, translated on the page.

In the Name of God, the Most Gracious, the Most Merciful. All praise is for God, the Lord of all worlds...

The words are a balm. They are not the start of a tribal story, but a universal declaration of love for the Creator of all that is. They feel less like an introduction and more like a key, turning in a lock deep within her soul.

Selah spends the night reading. She does not read from cover to cover, but searches, a lifetime of conditioning still half-expecting to find the "playbook of the enemy." Her fingers scan the table of contents, and a quiet shock ripples through her. The names are not strange. They are the names of her own spiritual family.

Her wonder grows as she turns to a chapter and reads of Musa (Moses). As her eyes scan the familiar story of his struggle with Pharaoh, a brief, warm flashback illuminates her mind:

She sees her own mother's hands, frail but steady, lighting the Shabbat candles. She hears the familiar Hebrew blessing, a soft melody in the quiet of their home.

The memory connects the foundation of her past to her present discovery with a thread of pure love.

She keeps reading, finding a chapter on 'Isa (Jesus), his miraculous birth and his powerful verbs of healing. Then she finds an entire chapter named for his mother, Maryam (Mary), honoring her with a reverence that takes Selah's breath away. This is not the book of the other. This is the story of her own prophets, her own sacred lineage. Her mind reels with a profound sense of awe and relief. Her internal monologue crystallizes with a beautiful, tearful realization:

"It is as if I have discovered a letter from a part of the family I never knew we had. The names are our names, the stories are our stories..."

Her reading is a profound comfort, a homecoming she never expected. But it also raises a thousand new questions. The structure, the poetic cadence, the context—it is all new. She recognizes the names, but she does not yet understand the grammar of this revelation.

In the morning light, she knows with perfect clarity what she must do. The Torah had required a guide, and God sent her Rabbi Elara. The Gospel had required a guide, and God sent her Sister Joan. She understands now that this final, clarifying recitation also requires a teacher. Her journey is not one of solitary reading in a library; it is, and has always been, one of sacred learning, heart to heart.

Her search leads her to a small, respected Islamic learning center nestled in a quiet street of the Old City. There, she meets her final, essential guide, Sheikha Imani. The Sheikha is a woman whose serenity is a palpable force, whose presence radiates a powerful stillness. Her eyes are full of a wisdom that seems both ancient and immediate, and they greet Selah with a gentle, knowing light, as if she has been expected all along.

As Selah enters the Sheikha's simple, book-lined study, a subtle sensory detail greets her: *a small vase on the desk holding a sprig of fresh rosemary,* the exact same scent from her mother's garden and the garden at Sister Joan's community. It is a beautiful, unspoken thread connecting her first source of love with her final guide.

Selah, clutching her translated copy of the Qur'an, feels a familiar hesitation. "Sheikha," she begins, her voice quiet. "I've been... reading this book."

Sheikha Imani smiles, a gesture of profound and gentle warmth. "A noble effort, my dear," she says, her voice as calm as still water. "But that is only a translation. The Qur'an is not a book; it is a *recitation.* It is meant to be heard."

The distinction lands with quiet power, shifting Selah's entire understanding. This is not a text to be studied like a manual; it is a song to be received by the heart.

"But before we begin," the Sheikha continues, her gaze full of a deep, loving compassion, "

We do not convert you to Islam, my dear; we awaken you to the Islam already in your soul."

Selah expresses her confusion, her journey through the beautiful truths of Judaism and Christianity, and now her arrival at what feels like a third, separate path. The Sheikha listens with perfect, patient love. When Selah is finished, the Sheikha does not offer a complicated answer. She offers a single verse. She guides Selah to a passage in the book she holds, to Qur'an 3:67.

Selah leans forward and reads the words that will complete the circle of her entire journey.

"'Abraham was neither a Jew nor a Christian, but he was... a Muslim (one who submits).'"

The words are a thunderclap of revelation in the quiet room. The final wall in her heart does not just crumble; it evaporates.

Sheikha Imani explains softly, "'Muslim' is not a tribal noun, Selah. It is the timeless verb describing anyone, from any age, who submits their will to the One God. Abraham was a submitter. Moses was a submitter. Jesus was a submitter. You have been learning this one, primordial verb your entire life."

As Selah processes this world-altering truth, her mind flashes with gratitude to the guide who made her heart ready for it. *A healed heart recognizes its Beloved's voice in any tongue,* she thinks, a silent thank you to Sister Joan.

A look of utter revelation washed over Selah's face... The energy is not one of conversion, but of breathtaking completion. The final thought in her mind is a whisper of pure, unadulterated awe:

"I haven't been converting... I've been remembering."

As the thought landed in her soul, a faint, beautiful sound began to drift through the window from somewhere in the city—the sound of the Adhan, the call to prayer. It was a sound that was no longer foreign, but a call home.

Episode 13: "A Heaven Without Walls"

The days with Sheikha Imani were like drinking cool water after a lifetime of thirst. A quiet bliss had settled in Selah's soul as she learned, a sense of homecoming that she had ached for. Her heart was at peace.

One sun-drenched afternoon, that peace was shattered. She was walking through the ancient, bustling streets of the Old City when she saw him—the elderly Jewish man from the community. He was speaking with a young, earnest tourist, who clutched a pamphlet like a shield.

Selah drew closer, and the tourist's words, spoken with a condescending pity, cut through the air. "But sir," the young man said, "unless you accept Jesus as your personal savior, your faith is invalid. I'm telling you this because I don't want you to be lost."

Selah watched as a shadow of deep, ancient pain passed over the old man's face. He did not argue. He simply gave a small, dignified nod and turned to walk away. The sight of his pained, dignified silence and the tourist's arrogant certainty reopened Selah's old wounds of "chosenness" and "replacement" with a fresh, sharp pain.

She went to Sheikha Imani, her heart troubled not for herself, but for the good, righteous man she had seen so casually dismissed.

"Sheikha," she began, her voice tight with an urgent need for clarity. "I see the beauty in all three paths. But I still see the walls. I see them everywhere. I see good people being told they are lost. What is the final truth? Who is saved? Does God have a chosen people, or not? I need to understand the blueprint for Heaven's walls."

Sheikha Imani listened, her serene expression acknowledging the depth of Selah's pain. "The mercy of God is a great river, Selah. Let us look at the channels He has already revealed," the Sheikha said. "What did the Torah teach you about the one who is not of your tribe?"

Selah's mind went back to her time with Rabbi Elara. "That you shall love the stranger as yourself".

"A beautiful, merciful verb," the Sheikha affirmed. "And the Gospel?"

"'To love your neighbor as yourself'".

"Another expression of the same Divine love," the Sheikha said. She then leaned forward, her voice imbued with a unifying power. **"You see, Selah, the revelations are not competing rivers fighting for space. The Torah and the Gospel are mighty rivers, carving the landscape of the soul with justice and mercy. The final recitation is not a storm that washes them away; it is the great, clarifying ocean into which they all flow, their essential truth preserved and protected."**

"But you are asking for the final, unambiguous statement," the Sheikha continued. "The verse that removes all doubt." She gestured to a Qur'an on the table. "Please, read."

She guided Selah to the Qur'an's explicit "Mercy Clause". Selah's finger traced the words as she read them aloud:

"'Indeed, those who believed and those who were Jews or Christians or Sabians—those who believed in God and the Last Day and did righteousness—will have their reward with their Lord, and no fear will there be concerning them, nor will they grieve'".

The verse landed in the quiet room with the force of pure, liberating light. Selah read it again, the words a balm on every wound of exclusion she had ever felt. She looked up at the Sheikha, her eyes wide with the dawning of a profound understanding.

"This is the essence of Islam's post-tribal vision," Sheikha Imani explained gently. "Paradise is not a private club for those who carry the right noun—'Jew,' 'Christian,' 'Muslim.' It is a home for those who perform the right verbs:

to believe in the One God and *to do* righteousness".

The wound healed. Not just for a day, but forever. In her mind, she heard a new thought, clear and bright:

It's not a new song... It echoes the song my own prophets have been singing for centuries. This thought then culminated in a whispered, revolutionary thesis, spoken aloud to herself: **"So, Paradise is not a noun you inherit; it is a verb you live"**. She saw with perfect clarity that the family of God was defined by action, not ancestry.

Later that day, Selah sought out the elderly Jewish man. She found him sitting alone on a bench in a quiet courtyard, looking disheartened.

She didn't preach or explain. She simply approached with a thermos of hot, sweet tea and a small plate with a piece of honey cake. She sat beside him, poured two cups, and offered him one. A silent, loving verb of companionship that transcended any wall. Her heart was now, finally, unwalled.

He looked at her, his tired eyes filled with a gentle surprise. He took the cup. They sat for a long moment in a comfortable, healing silence. After a final sip of tea, he turned to her, his eyes full of ancient wisdom and gentle gratitude, and offered the reciprocal blessing:

"It is good to sit with a righteous soul."

His words landed in her heart, a perfect, validating echo of the verse she had just learned. They shared a quiet, comfortable silence as the Jerusalem sun cast long, golden shadows, two righteous souls at peace.

Episode 14: "The Broken Flow"

A profound peace had settled in Selah's heart, a quiet bliss born from the discovery of a heaven without walls. She walked the ancient streets of Jerusalem with new eyes, seeing not a city of divisions, but a city of shared humanity. She saw the love in the eyes of a mother wearing a hijab, the devotion in the prayers of a man wearing a kippah, the charity in the hands of a nun serving soup.

But her peace was disturbed by a new, logical, and painful question. She also saw the walls—both physical and invisible—that still divided the city's faithful. Her internal monologue was a constant, troubled prayer:

If the truth is so beautifully unified, why is the world so fractured? If all the rivers flow to one ocean, why do we insist on building dams? Why isn't this good news shared?

She brought this heartfelt question to Sheikha Imani, her frustration evident in her voice. "Sheikha, I feel like I'm holding a cure for a sickness, but I see the sickness everywhere, and no one is sharing the cure."

Sheikha Imani's gaze was serene and full of understanding. "You have just discovered the most important and most wounded verb in our tradition, my dear. The verb of *Da'wah*."

"The world has taught you that *Da'wah* is 'proselytizing' or 'conversion'—nouns of conquest," the Sheikha explained. "But in its pure form, it is the gentle verb of 'inviting.' Of 'healing.' This is the truth you have already learned in your soul: that to truly submit is to nurture your being. You do not force a thirsty person to drink, my dear. You simply show them where the well is."

Awe filled Selah's face. "If it's that simple and beautiful," she asked, "what happened? Why did it stop?"

A shadow of sorrow passed over the Sheikha's features. "Because the river of revelation has always flowed through the landscape of human power," she said, her voice imbued with a historian's precision and a believer's sorrow. She began to reveal the tragic history of how the verb of sharing the Divine invitation was silenced by politics and empire.

As she spoke, her words were interwoven with brief, haunting, and poetic visual flashes, half-second memories from the river of history itself:

"The gentle invitation of Moses was hardened into a noun of tribal chosenness, used to justify the power of kings..." *A quick flash of a **Roman standard with an eagle standing before the Second Temple**, a symbol of imperial power overshadowing sacred space.*

"...the radical, enemy-loving verb of Jesus was frozen into the noun of 'Christendom'..." *A flash of a **Crusader's banner, the cross held like a weapon, not a symbol of sacrifice**, glinting under a harsh sun.*

"...and the pure, universal call of Islam was, for a time, silenced by the noise of 'caliphate' and conquest."

*A flash of a **caliph's opulent, golden throne, a stark contrast to the Prophet's humble mat**, a symbol of worldly power replacing prophetic humility.*

These visuals made the tragedy of the "broken flow" a visceral, emotional experience for Selah, not just an intellectual one. She saw how the pure "river of faith began to stagnate" behind man-made walls.

As Selah listened to this painful history, the final, crucial piece of the trilogy's entire puzzle clicked into place.

Sheikha Imani's voice was now a gentle but piercing whisper. **"Da'wah is the verb of showing a soul the well. Conquest is the noun of forcing them to drink."**

The words landed, and Selah saw the direct correlation between the silencing of this verb and the rise of noun-based nationalism. Her internal monologue was sharp, clear, and devastating:

"So the God of Nouns wasn't a theological mistake. It was a political one. It was born when the prophets were silenced by the kings."

She saw, for the first time, the historical root of the very thing she had been fighting.

Selah was left feeling the immense weight of this history, a sense of hopelessness at the scale of the corruption. "So the flow is broken," she said, her voice flat with despair. "The dams won."

"No, my child," Sheikha Imani said, her serenity returning like the sun after a storm. "The flow was never truly broken. Empires and politicians tried to dam the river, but the true verb of *Da'wah* simply went underground. It continued not in the courts of kings, but in the quiet, loving actions of the righteous."

She leaned forward, her eyes locking with Selah's, her next words a symphony of the entire trilogy:

"It continued in a Rabbi's patient teaching to a broken soldier. In a Sister's humble service that opened a wounded heart. In a young woman sharing tea with a lonely old man."

The despair vanished from Selah's face, replaced by a look of dawning, breathtaking realization and renewed purpose. She understands. She is not outside the story; she is the continuation of the "unbroken flow." Her mission is becoming clear. As these words land, she looks down at her own hands, then reaches out and touches a single, living leaf on a plant in the Sheikha's garden—a quiet, physical connection to the life force she has now inherited.

Episode 15: "One God, One Will, Three Expressions"

Selah is in a state of calm clarity, the turmoil of her past replaced by a deep, intellectual peace. She has been studying, integrating, and a final, crucial question has surfaced—not from a place of pain, but from a place of awe.

She turns to the Sheikha, her gaze direct and full of earnest curiosity. "I understand the history now," she begins. "I see how politics broke the flow. But the rivers themselves... the Torah, the Gospel, the Qur'an... they feel so different. Their laws, their languages, their focus. How can they be from one source if they don't always say the same thing? How can they be one will?"

Sheikha Imani smiles, a look of profound, loving recognition in her eyes. This is the final door to be unlocked.

"Selah, God is the most perfect teacher," she begins, her voice as gentle as the morning light. "A loving parent gives their young child simple, firm rules for safety and community. As that child becomes a teenager, the rules evolve, focusing more on internal character. When the child is a mature adult, the relationship becomes a contract of mutual love and trust. The parent is the same. The love is the same. But the expression of that love evolves to meet the needs of the one who is growing. The Torah, Gospel, and Qur'an are like this: an evolving contract from a single, loving God".

Sheikha Imani respectfully and lovingly guides Selah through the unique role of each revelation within this evolving contract, elevating the lesson with breathtaking metaphorical power.

"Allow me to show you how each revelation played its part, the Torah," she explains, "was the foundational contract, Selah. The grammar of Justice. Our Torah was not replaced; it was honored as the **foundation stone upon which the whole cathedral was built.**"

"Then came the personal evolution," she continues, her voice softening, "the grammar of Mercy.

The Gospel was the heart, installed to pump the blood of Mercy through the body of the Law."

"And the final, universal expression," she concludes, her voice full of a gentle finality, "is the grammar of Submission. **The Qur'an is the final architectural drawing that reveals how the foundation and the heart were always part of the same, perfect design."**

As Selah listens, the entire journey—from Rabbi Elara's dusty study to Sister Joan's sunlit garden to this quiet, fragrant room—coalesces into a single, breathtaking truth. She finally grasps the full "God of Verbs Vs. God of Nouns" Trilogy in its entirety. The different expressions were not contradictions; they were different lessons from the same, perfect Teacher.

Her eyes fill with tears of pure, intellectual and spiritual joy. She looks at the Sheikha, her voice a whisper of profound discovery.

"Obey. Love. Submit. Three verbs. One Will."

Selah was now in a state of profound, unshakable peace... In that single, silent touch, the three rivers of revelation flowed together under her hand, becoming one ocean, one story, from one God. The seeking is over. The integration is complete.

Selah that evening, sitting at her own small desk. On it, she has placed her three books—the Torah, the New Testament, and the Qur'an. She looks at them not as a collection of competing texts, but as three beautiful, seamlessly bound volumes of a single, unfolding Divine Trilogy.

After a moment of profound, peaceful contemplation, she slowly and reverently **places her hand over all three books at once, her palm covering the Tanakh, the New Testament, and the Qur'an without distinction.** This single, silent action is a physical declaration that for her, they are now one story, from one God. Her mission is no longer just a feeling; it is a fully formed, theologically complete understanding, ready to be lived.

Episode 16: "Rivers to the Ocean"

Selah in a state of integrated peace, is leading a small study group in the community center's garden, a circle of Jewish, Christian, and Muslim women around her, her voice a calm and gentle thread weaving between the Torah, the Gospel, and the Qur'an. Her peace is real, her wholeness earned.

Her phone vibrates on the table. She excuses herself, and the single word from the nurse on the other end of the line—"Selah..."—is all it takes.

The news shatters her peace, but not her foundation. The grief is immense, a sudden, sharp intake of breath that threatens to steal the air from her lungs. But underneath it, her response is one of clear, focused purpose. Her final mission is born not from a plan, but from a desperate, loving need: she must bring the whole of God's mercy—the Justice, the Love, and the Submission she has learned—to her mother as a final, living gift.

What follows is a powerful, urgent journey across the holy city, a gathering of the rivers of mercy.

She finds Rabbi Elara in the dusty, quiet light of the Synagogue's library. The Rabbi sees the look on Selah's face and knows immediately. As Selah begins her plea, her voice choked with emotion, a brief, poignant flashback pierces her mind:

Selah's mother, younger but hollowed by grief, lifting the simple cotton sheet to cover the mirror in their home. The memory gives her words a raw, heart-wrenching power. "Rabbi, please. You must come. She is going. I need her to feel the foundation of your Justice, the strength of the covenant that held her all her life."

Next, she finds Sister Joan tending to a patient. When they are alone, her request is just as heartfelt. "Sister, please. I need her to feel the grace of your Mercy, the radical love that heals the deepest wounds." Sister Joan simply takes off her apron, her eyes already saying yes.

Finally, she arrives at the serene quiet of Sheikha Imani's study. Her voice is now a whisper, full of a sacred awe for what she is about to ask. "Sheikha, I need her to feel the peace of your Submission, the final, beautiful surrender to the One."

The three guides meet for the first time, not in a grand hall, but in the humble, love-worn living room of Selah's apartment. The air is still, charged with the sacred weight of impending mortality. Sheikha Imani pours three small glasses of mint tea, the fragrant steam rising like a shared prayer. For a moment, they are simply three women, holding the warmth of the glasses in their hands.

Rabbi Elara is the first to speak, her voice a soft melody against the quiet hum of the city outside. "The soul," she says, looking into her glass, "is like a flame. It never dies; it is only returned to the great fire from which it came. I have spent my life teaching this. But to see it in one so young… to see our Selah guide her own mother home… it is a lesson that teaches the teacher."

Sister Joan nods, a compassionate, weary smile touching her lips. "She is a soldier to the last, isn't she? I taught her that the Gospel was a set of orders for a different kind of war. I never imagined her final mission would be this. To command a soul, with love, to stand down and be at peace." She shakes her head in gentle wonder. "She learned to forgive the unforgivable in herself. Now she is using that grace to face the unfaceable for her mother."

Sheikha Imani looks from the Rabbi to the Sister, her gaze a pool of serene acceptance. "You both gave her such beautiful verbs," she says, her voice calm as still water. "You gave her *lashuv*, to turn. You gave her *agape*, to love. You prepared the vessel. All that was left was for her to learn *taslim*, to submit. Not in defeat, but in peace." She meets their eyes. "Her soul was never broken. It was just… unfinished. And now, because of the rivers you tended, she is ready to guide her mother to the ocean."

They sit in a comfortable, knowing silence, the space between them filled not with doctrine, but with a profound, shared love for the student who had become the master. Just before they rise, Rabbi Elara reaches out and places her hand over Sister Joan's. Sheikha Imani gently covers them both. Three hands, from three worlds, resting together. A silent, universal understanding is exchanged: a nod of respect, a shared look of compassion, a mutual recognition of the sacred, human task before them. This wordless moment of unity speaks volumes, a powerful, emotional bridge that every soul can cross.

The three guides, followed by Selah, enter the mother's quiet room. The air is thick with reverence. This is the living embodiment of the theology. As they begin, Selah's heart understands the moment in a flash of Divine clarity:

They were not surrendering their traditions; they were offering them to the One God as a single, unified gift.

Rabbi Elara steps into the quiet reverence of the bedside. She lays a hand on her friend's forehead, and from her lips flows the ancient river of the covenant—a blessing in soft, melodic Hebrew, each word a stone of timeless Justice paving the soul's path home.

Then Sister Joan comes forward, taking the mother's frail hand in both of her own. Her prayer is a quiet cascade of English, a river of radical Mercy poured out, washing over the room with a grace that makes the air feel soft.

Finally, Sheikha Imani stands beside Selah, a comforting hand on her shoulder, her voice a third river of perfect, serene Arabic, reciting the Qur'an's promise of the soul returning to its Lord, a sound as peaceful and inevitable as the tide.

Three languages, three prayers, one God. It is not a chorus of conflict, but a single, harmonious symphony of faith.

In the peaceful aftermath of the blessing, Selah's mother opens her eyes with a profound and sudden lucidity. She looks at Selah, and then at the three guides standing together. A faint, beautiful smile touches her lips.

Her voice is a fragile whisper, but it is full of a final, loving command.

"Selah... uncover the mirrors."

With tears of sorrow and joy streaming down her face, Selah walks to the mirror above the dresser and finally, after all these years, removes the cloth. The reflection in the mirror, a portrait of **three**

rivers of mercy reflecting one healed soul, proving the Oneness of the ocean. In the glass, we see Selah, no longer a broken soldier but a whole and healed soul, standing with her peaceful mother, and flanked by the three faces of the single, merciful God she has come to know. It is the perfect, final portrait of her completed journey.

As she looks at this image, a final realization crystallizes in her heart. *In the end, all the beautiful nouns—Torah, Gospel, Qur'an— had dissolved into one perfect verb: to love. And as she looked at the reflection, she knew what she had just done. She hadn't just convened a council. She had orchestrated a miracle.*

Episode 17: "The Living Covenant"

In the days following her mother's peaceful passing, Selah sat *shiva*, but the atmosphere was completely different from the suffocating grief that began Selah's path. The mirrors in the home were now uncovered, and the room was filled with a soft, gentle light that seemed to emanate from the very walls. The air was not heavy with unspoken sorrow, but alive with the quiet hum of community.

Friends from all three of Selah's worlds came to pay their respects. The elderly Jewish man, his eyes full of a deep, knowing peace, sat and shared a silent cup of tea. A few members from Sister Joan's center arrived with a warm meal, their presence a gentle comfort. The woman in the hijab whom Selah saw on her first day at the center came and offered a quiet, heartfelt prayer. The feeling was one of profound peace and unity. The grief was real, but it was a sweet sorrow, bathed in the light of the blessings Selah had witnessed.

After the final day of *shiva*, as Selah lovingly and peacefully sorted through her mother's belongings, she found a small, elegant box tucked away in a drawer of linens. Inside, nestled on a bed of faded velvet, are four envelopes, sealed and addressed in her mother's familiar, frail handwriting. Three were addressed to: "Rabbi Elara," "Sister Joan," and "Sheikha Imani." The fourth simply said: "Selah." A wave of profound love washed over Selah. She understood instantly. Her mother, in her final days of lucidity, had performed one last act of grace. Selah had been entrusted with her mother's final act of gratitude, her final verbs.

Her journey to deliver the letters became a final, gentle pilgrimage to her guides. She was not coming with questions, but with a gift.

Her first visit was to Rabbi Elara in the quiet of her study. The Rabbi read the letter, her hand coming to her mouth as she wept with quiet, profound joy. She looked up at Selah, her eyes shining. "May the God of our fathers and mothers bless the path you walk, my child. You have honored us all."

From the Synagogue, her path led her to the sunlit garden of the community center. Joan read the letter with a radiant smile that lit up her entire face. She folded the page, placed a hand on Selah's arm, and said, "Your mother understood the Gospel perfectly: it is love."

Her final stop was the serene stillness of the Islamic center. The Sheikha read the letter, closed her eyes, and touched it to her heart. She looked at Selah with a deep, peaceful reverence. "Her soul submitted so beautifully. She is with her Lord."

Each meeting was a quiet, loving farewell, a passing of the torch from the mentors to their now-graduated student.

Selah returned to the quiet of her own home as the sun was setting, casting a warm, golden glow through the windows. She sat and, with a hand that was no longer trembling but perfectly steady, she opened the final letter, the one addressed to her. As her eyes traced the familiar, frail handwriting, her mother's voice seemed to fill the quiet room, clear and full of love, speaking the words in her heart.

"My dearest Selah, my light. If you are reading this, I am at peace in a place where there are no more covered mirrors. I have watched you journey from a brokenness I could not heal to a wholeness that healed even me. You were my greatest mitzvah, my most beautiful prayer."

Selah's tears fell silently onto the page.

"That last day... the miracle you brought into my room... I saw it all. You brought all of God's mercy into one room for me. Now, you must be that room for the world. The covenant is not in a book anymore, my love. You are the Living Covenant now. Go, and be a blessing."

With her mother's final words echoing in her heart, Selah took the first concrete step of her new, active mission. She sat at her desk, the letter held gently in her hand. She pulled out a fresh piece of paper and, after a moment of quiet, prayerful contemplation, she began to write.

Her pen formed a title at the top of the page: *"The Jerusalem Project: A Home for the Verbs."*

A look of profound peace and determination settled on her features. She was no longer a seeker, but a founder; an architect of unity, ready for the work that was to come.

Episode 18: "The Final Verb"

Selah stands before a derelict, forgotten building in a neighborhood that lies at the seam of Jerusalem's three quarters. Its walls are scarred with the graffiti of division, its windows are broken, but in the morning light, Selah sees only potential. She holds the blueprint for "The Jerusalem Project."

She is not alone. With her are the quiet heroes of her journey—the elderly Jewish man, his eyes bright with hope; members from Sister Joan's Christian community, their sleeves already rolled up; and new friends from the Islamic center, their faces full of a calm resolve. There are no speeches. There is no ceremony. Selah simply unrolls the blueprint on the hood of a dusty car, and together, they begin the first verb: *to build*.

The weeks that followed were a blur of joyful, sacred work... The "House of the Verbs" opened its doors, a living symphony of the trilogy's thesis. It was not a place for debate, but a place for doing... Her life was now a continuous, open invitation...

The derelict building is transformed, not by contractors, but by a community. We see a multi-faith group of volunteers working side-by-side. We see hammering and painting and gardening, and through it all, we see laughter and shared meals. The energy is one of pure, unadulterated, shared purpose.

A simple, beautiful, hand-carved sign is raised above the newly painted doorway. It is written in three languages, the words flowing together: **Beit HaPe'el. The House of the Verbs. Bayt al-Fi'l.**

We see a shared kitchen where a woman in a hijab and a woman in a kippah are laughing as they cook together, sharing recipes. We see a classroom where a Christian volunteer patiently teaches Hebrew to a small group of excited Arab children. We see a workshop where an old Palestinian man, a master carpenter, teaches a group of Jewish teenagers how to repair a broken chair.

And in the middle of it all, we see them: Rabbi Elara, Sister Joan, and Sheikha Imani. They are not lecturers or leaders here. They are joyful participants, sipping tea, sharing in the work, their eyes watching Selah with a profound, tearful pride.

The final communal takes place in the newly planted garden. Selah is with a small group of Jewish, Christian, and Muslim children. Together, their small hands working in the dark, rich soil, they are planting a single olive sapling—a tiny, hopeful verb of peace.

One of the children, a little girl with wide, curious eyes, asks the question that has haunted this land for centuries. "Who does this tree belong to?"

Selah stops. She looks at their innocent, questioning faces, and with a gentle, loving smile that holds all the wisdom she has earned, she delivers the trilogy's final, beautiful piece of dialogue:

"We will not argue who owns the land. We will plant verbs in it together."

The day is over. The "House of the Verbs" is quiet. Selah is alone on the rooftop, looking out at the holy city as the sun sets. In the soft twilight, the sounds of the Adhan, the distant ringing of Church bells, and the faint, soulful call of a shofar begin to rise, blending into a single, harmonious melody.

We hear her final, internal thoughts, a quiet summary of her entire journey:

"In the beginning, my hands trembled with a wound. Then they learned to serve. Then to heal. Then to pray. Now... they plant."

She turns from the view. In the center of the rooftop, she lays down a small, simple prayer rug. In a moment of perfect peace, complete submission, and profound gratitude, she enters into *sajdah*—the final, quiet, perfect verb, the ultimate physical expression of a soul that is finally, completely, and eternally home. Her life is the Living Covenant. The story ends not with a conclusion, but with a continuous, open invitation to you to begin their own journey from noun to verb.

An Afterword from Selah

It has been ten years since we first opened the doors to *The Jerusalem Project: A Home for the Verbs*. The olive tree we planted with the children that first day has grown strong, its roots deep in the contested and holy soil of this city. It offers shade to all, asking nothing in return.

Our "House" has become many houses — in places of pain and places of peace, from the heart of Africa to the suburbs of America. The work is the same everywhere. We do not debate the nouns that divide us. We live the verbs that unite us — feeding, building, listening, healing, forgiving, loving.

From a Rabbi, I learned tikkun olam — the mending of the world. From a Sister, that the Gospel is love in action. I learned from a Sheikha that true submission is the stewardship of God's family. I have learned that all three are the same.

The covenant is not bound in a book, but in the bending of a back to lift another. It is in the trembling hand that steadies another. It is in the verb. Always the verb.

And now, I pass this to you. The path does not end here, for there are living bridges that carry this work forward:

You are not reading this by accident. The same unseen Hand that writes the stars may have placed this book in yours. If your heart stirs, act. Do not let faith remain an idea. Carry it into your home, your street, your workplace — into the faces of others where God waits to be met.

My mother, may God have mercy on her soul, left me with a final charge. Now, as my last act in this story, I pass it to you: Look at your life. Look closely — at your life, your hands, the world before you.

You are the Living Covenant now – walk it, breathe it, be a blessing

With Love,

Selah

If you seek to walk further on this path, join the hands that are already building. At **IslamicRecovery.com**, faith becomes a place of healing. At **IslamSchool.com**, learning becomes a verb. Jazak Allah Khair

Made in the USA
Middletown, DE
12 November 2025

20392411R00038